PSYCHODYNAMICS & CATHARSIS

PSYCHODYNAMICS & CATHARSIS

HOW TO DEAL WITH SOCIAL PROBLEMS

Dr. Keith Gavin

Copyright © 2020 by Dr. Keith Gavin.

Library of Congress Control Number:	2020909554
ISBN: Hardcover	978-1-9845-8076-4
Softcover	978-1-9845-8075-7
eBook	978-1-9845-8074-0

All rights reserved. No part of this book may be reproduced or transmitted in any form or by any means, electronic or mechanical, including photocopying, recording, or by any information storage and retrieval system, without permission in writing from the copyright owner.

Any people depicted in stock imagery provided by Getty Images are models, and such images are being used for illustrative purposes only.
Certain stock imagery © Getty Images.

Print information available on the last page.

Rev. date: 05/26/2020

To order additional copies of this book, contact:
Xlibris
1-888-795-4274
www.Xlibris.com
Orders@Xlibris.com
814459

CONTENTS

Society Pressure 1

Biblical Mis-Guidance 8

Economic Conditions 13

Lack of Leadership in the Communities 17

Mental Health Concern 22

Problem in the Community 30

Lack of Correct Education 35

Cognitive Thinking 40

Political Power 44

Balancing & Debt 48

Reference 53

About the Author 55

SOCIETY PRESSURE

WHEN LOOKING AT the issues, which we have in this society we have many communication issues our communities are in trouble due to the pressures to seek education and jobs that seems as thou they exist but really are difficult to obtain. Some of the deeper problems and social conditions that has divide the communities and citizens in the country are racial and social dissonance when the body of people are distant and keep from coming together. Many of our children are told go to school and pursue an education, to help them to obtain better jobs. Then they find out, that is not, the case, and they find out that many people are fighting for work and opportunities. The social pressure and issues that we must deal with are the deeper social issues, economic, and political conditions that have been interjected into the mindset and social construct of our nation.

Slavery was a social pressure, which used the physical labor of Africans and others. This was wrong in this society and abroad. Germany during the holocaust and the African slavery capture as well the passage to the America's was similar. Both ethnic people groups had deep social issues that created social pressures that still affect the psyche of men and women today. Because a group believed that by using African people do the physical work by containing them in ships and creating laws, that they knew that group could not change, they knew it was also wrong. African/ black Americans did and still do not have enough political power to change the laws in their communities and social surroundings.

The people group who are creating and developing the laws are only making laws that helps their people lift up while they keep others down. This ultimately creates social pressure and distrust in the society. The people who believe they are the major majority are keeping and controlling the social factors, because they believe that others need to fit their social norms in the society. It has caused mistrust and created a hate relationship in the heart of others whom are looking to understand the deeper social needs. What if the laws were changed and the ones who believe where in charge switch places how do you think they would feel? This was the thought after reconstruction which they created to make economic distance between blacks and whites.

How can the group that feel slighted in the society change the laws when they are kept socially despondent from the power because of legislation? Just look at the representatives and congressional seats in each district and ask yourself what is the problem? If a group of people are not able to create legal change in the way laws have been developed or created then how do they compete in the society and make those changes. The laws and the political offices must be balanced. When the history and the application of the truth has been stifled for years and changed to fit the needs of the justice system that was created for only one group to benefit from then how can the people who seek justice receive fair treatment from the system. "A system cannot fail those it was never meant to protect" - W.E.B. Du Bois

This created a mental model for others to treat the disenfranchised individual like second class citizens within the local communities and it made the social pressures more difficult to maneuver and the social class environment was then created in the American society. How do you deal with the social problems in the community and nation when the cards have been stacked? Reader take note if the laws that govern our nation is changed and dealt with then the economy we have will collapse. This is one of the problems that Martin Luther king was dealing with nullification and interposition.

Let's take a good look at the issues, the laws were enacted to govern behavior, slavery was one of those process they were used after they annihilated the American Indian. This was a very horrendous time in the American society and each ethnic group that came into the country treated others who were not them like they were animals. The society used to kill African American people and hung them from trees. This enactment created a psychological and diabolical process within the psychosis of African American people during the early 1930s and 1950s in rural townships throughout the south. How does the law deal with this process in the society, we call fair and just? It created a hysteria and phobia of the social justice system for people of color.

When Antigone, felt as thou she would defy the edict of Creon which was wrong in her sight. The law was sought for change and she went against his law. This is something that African Americans must truly understand and make the political and social changes in the law by occupying the seats and changing the playing field. What has happened in the political field is that the ones in power help those hold on to the seats lower than them to keep rule over them.

When the society where one lives is not conducive to their living standards and styles then political and social correctives must prevail using the heart and mind God gave them. Any group who is use to the underclass must understand the games that are played on them to survive and begin to think how to adapt to the changes and relook at the structure. When the social mirror is turned inside out and the people that made the laws fit only one group and neglect others who live in the communities. There is no equality in the north and the south, they are both the same it seems like times are better but there is an economic barrier placed somewhere in the midst.

If the playing field is the same then why are the economic status of blacks different than any other group. They been in America for 400 years and still cannot own franchises or plazas. The people who created the mayhem don't like what they see and want to change the laws to get rid of the people they trained to be like them. They do not have no more use for them, so they make them to hate themselves and fear unity. In the Bible, in Genesis (11 vs 6 d) says that if they come together, nothing they do could be restrained.

Once again, the people need a leader to lead them out of the land of this new Egypt. Now that the world is looking at what they have created that mirror is not showing a good picture. We cannot accept the facts and lies anymore; we must change the status quo (mess where in). The societies pressure is so bad and it seems like the laws are breaking down in the local communities and location where the people are living. The reality is that they are unjust and do not fit in our society because the people who constructed the laws had bad intentions when they were created. The ones who created the problems are afraid that they will be subjected to the same laws they have imposed on the mass majority and are scared that what they have done is going to be reversed.

The legislation must be changed to adequately fit the society and fairness of the prosperity of the nation that everyone is supposed to enjoy. If the laws and the southern strategies policies was not exposed to the world it would have kept the enactment of slavery alive. Yes, I know the jails are full of people that they no longer need in the society as it seems. The southern strategies shaped the laws of the mind of only one group of people to keep other groups down this is and has been the polices of the individuals who have been govern the communities.

If you are not part of the process of change then how can the progress be changed and if the laws are only one sided. Then how can the people who may never be lifted form the poverty ever get an opportunity to be a full productive citizen. The social structure must be changed and the laws must be equal if the underclass will have an opportunity to compete in the world they live. The question remains are you ready to make that change and get involved in the process of change for your community and country.

The white society bereded discourse and mistrust for many years and only helped the ones who stole the land and money from those who had the ideas to construct the nation. The plans and ideas were stolen, recipes for cooking, manufacturing ideas for cars and other things that people have never been paid for in the communities. Many people were manipulated out of their royalties and life savings trusting in slick individuals who only had it out for themselves and their own families. This is called brainwashed when you believe that someone can tell you that they will look out for your best interest and take your things and you sign them over to them to give you a profit.

The issues in the society that keeps the people down will create depression in the community in mental health they will look at the biopsychosocial process to figure out what has caused the problems and put a charge to it, today I am giving it to you free of charge all you have to do is read this chapter and book.

The social construct and the community issues need to be overhauled and relooked even the economic disparities and distribution of funds in the community. Must be dealt with by having the people in that community explain what they need in their community which helps them to survive, Jobs, adequate health care, food and training programs in the community then the social pressures and mental health issues as well as how they cognitively deal with social issues can be better dealt with to identify the more critical concerns they are faced with daily. The question that come up are we still governed by the slave codes?

Change must come from the people in the community and if they do not understand the issues; then how do they deal with the issues from a community standpoint. African Americans must can come together and brainstorm how to identify the problems and assist each other in dealing with the greater deeper issues. Each community must have and create a think-tank to sharpen the resolve and make an impact in their community.

"Would Any White Person Trade Places with A Negro in America"

NOTES

BIBLICAL MIS-GUIDANCE

THE INFORMATION THAT was given to the disinherited people was watered down and given to them during the transatlantic slave trade. They were chained and packed in a ship like sardines, young boys were rapped and young girls sexually abused. Taken to west indies and Jamaica to work the plantations while being treated bad and men were rapped Infront of other slaves by the keepers in the butt. They called this method buck busting; now today young black men wear their pants down around their but with their underwear. Forensic psychology explains to us that men have been broken and the police no longer need to worry about them.

They changed the meanings and imagines of the ones who connected the truth to the masses to assist themselves and confused the people whom it was intended. The Bible was originally translated from Arabic; from the Talmud, which gave away to the correct information that was to be presented but somehow it was revised to change the truth and has cause confusion in the minds of the people who transported the slaves to this peninsula. Did blacks come here with no religion and no God; they were born like everyone else.

Now that the mental thoughts and economic plight of the people has been altered the guidance from the Bible was taught and has dimmed the thinking of a group of people and caused them to be lazy in their action. When the intended individuals understand better the detriment of the information shared with them from the captor's prospector then they will understand how to combat the information and take that pressure off their mind. If the correct information is to be given and the information relooked at closely is taken in and revised to meet the social and economic needs of the people it was intended for then the power and economic balance can be understood better in the world we live. This is one of the problems when dealing with social problems in the communities that many African Americans are having problems with and why they are not working together sharing in the wealth of this nation. Instead they are on the bottom feeding the establishment with their skills and money and not benefiting for their own economic labor. They do not own anything other than a car and some shoes that are overpriced. The Bible explains to the masses if correctly shared that everything is owned by the great architect, the supreme being.

The Biblical text states that God brought them up out of the land of Egypt, out of the house of bondage. How then do the masses come up with "Israel" being the place of the original origin? This is part of the confusion that has been delivered to the masses. If Jesus, his mother, and Joseph was told to go and hide in Egypt; he must have looked like the people he was hiding among. This shows you that if critical information is withheld from individuals and the evidence is deluded it can cause some psychodynamic conditions to enter the psyche and eventually change the threshold of the persons mindset.

The best technique to deal with this dynamic and to dissolve the pressure from the mis-educated concepts is to go to the places and ask critical and crucial questions to gain a better understand of the issues first hand. This means that in order to breakdown the deceptions and upload the truth you will have to travel back in time to gain the experience in real time. Once this has been established it will open your eyes and mind to the lies told to you that they have progenerated through the Biblical context.

The greatest determent that happen to people of color was done in two parts; 1) Slavery, and 2) Colonialism engages in the process, to impose religion, economics, and medicinal practices on the individuals under their rule and control. Colonialism is the relationship of domination of indigenous by foreign invaders where the latter rule in pursuit of their interests. When looking at slavery it is a system in which principles of property and laws are applied to people, denying individuals to own, buy and land but selling other individuals, as a form of property.

The individuals who controlled and studied the people's mindset and ways of learning began to twist and lie to the officials in that environment to change how they advance in their own society. This is an educational teaching that the Biblical scholars has constructed in the religious thinking of the indigent people of a community and nation. Biblical misguidance is done to change how a group believes in their own liberation. This pressure is part of the problem in the society where many people live in everyday and by understanding the dynamics of the situation. It is critical that a group of cognitive thinkers begin to re-educate those whom have been affected by this way of thinking so they can wake up. God is the ultimate sustainer, who is our refuge in the time of trouble, the rock of our comfort, the lily in the valley, the bright morning star; he is our deliverer whom we shall call on. He is the wind beneath our wings, he is the wind we feel and the love we share, he is the one whom we look to in the time of joy from our pain. God is right and never wrong, so there is no need to doubt him or deny the power of him that dwells within, we are to hold on to God's unchanging hand and he will take care of us. When fire comes God is there, when the earth starts to shake God is there, when the night grows dreary and the skies get gray God is there, for God is everywhere all you have to do is don't worry, for he will take care of you.

We must meet God on the road, for he is waiting for us to come up with new and fresh ideas and strategies, God wants you to know that he is still in control or he has theocracy. God wants to remind you that we must mark our goals, plan our direction, and set out to meet him on the road of struggle. Who is on the Lords side? Do we trust God, at his word, that he will never leave us or forsake us, and what role do we play in the ecumenical arena, meaning the economy of God. We cannot build safely on false foundations, for truth makes a new creature, in whom old things pass away and all things will become new.

NOTES

ECONOMIC CONDITIONS

WHEN THE UNDERCLASS has been forgotten and the masses of people have risen above the social circumstances then the distribution of wealth has only been shared with others. The economic conditions in many places are not evenly distributed it will create a social underclass in any thriving society.

The only way to deal with this problem is to understand the economic power of commerce, by studying the products and buying power of the social class. If these economic issues are to be dealt with then the products and people in that community must find an outlet and create an economic power structure to secure their own economic freedom. Colonialism damaged the mindset of the individual in many areas and has caused a social breakdown of the economics as well the social problems we find today in the world in which many black live. By identifying the economic problem, you will have to look at the corruption and distribution of the funds to figure out the deeper problems.

You will probably find out that the masses are under-educated and lack simple reading and social skills to compete in their own environment. This is part of how colonialism has caused discord in many of the areas where darker people are at and it has caused problems in every nation and the communities where people of color has been placed over the years.

The questions that will arise from this study and eye-opening concept when uncovering the deep-seated issues of colonialism is understanding the slave trade and how it affected the places where darker people reside. Economics is always a factor in any community and world order. By following the distribution and allocation of the funds it will help to clarify many of the social issues and problems blacks and others have faced over the centuries and help us to shift the economic distribution. The key to dealing with the issues and movement of economics lay in understanding the Biblical model and digging into how the individuals took what God has already done and showed Africans. They came with economic skills teaching other nations how to save money using African money skills, where they went through Europe showing them how to manage their funds. Their was a man who many blacks were not told about who defied the establishment when it came to money. Paul Cuffe (1759-1817) was the richest African American in the United States during the early 1800's, but never stopped championing the cause of better conditions for his people. By 1811, Paul Cuffe felt that if blacks were to be treated with disrespect then he would leave the United States and go back to Africa, this is what many blacks have done in those years. If blacks in America was considered a second-class citizen, then emigration back to Africa was the only answer for Black social, economic, and political self-determination.

When digging in the archives of history I realized that psychodynamics and catharsis was really a issue that many blacks needed to understand in order for them to snap out of the dream that the system has trapped them in education and economics. Is the key to getting out of mental slavery here in the United States and share it with our brothers and sisters in Africa. The economic conditions for many blacks in the United States have been very hard and if they would learn how to work together and build an economic platform, they will rise out of the poverty-stricken state that the system keep trying to put them in every day. In the Bible is the key and the information to wealth is in it then it is up to the preachers and financial students to share with us how to read the recipe. God is always with us he was with us during the slave passage, he has been with us during the riots and lynching's even when the banks crashed in 1929. We must begin to spend our money with our own institution and use One United bank and change how we move our power in the community.

NOTES

LACK OF LEADERSHIP IN THE COMMUNITIES

LACK OF LEADERSHIP is hindered because the information given to the masses of people has been stifled and re-transmitted to cause division. Many of the leaders that have been given to the masses have been killed or placed into our community by the upper class to keep the masses subdued. When there is one who upraises against the masses, power holders will smear their name scandalize them and find something to discredit them.

This occurs many times in the black communities and other countries where People of color reside. Lack of Control and opportunities in the community causes psychodynamic issues, this has been building up for years, and it has to be dealt with in the world we live. It is essential to understand that when a group of people who have been mentally abused for centuries and decades are placed in an environment to succeed how will they with no economic support and training concur the obstacles they face every day.

Where are the leaders and the trainers? Who will take up the task to explain to the lost that the issues and problems are built in the educational methods and economic structures placed in the laws they do not control? Many different groups have risen above their circumstances and become part of the elite class in the communities they occupy. What happen to the slaves and the re-educated individual why have the rubber stamp and the check been bounced when it comes to the black communities. Those who have been in charge for years and in leadership positions has created a system that holds most of the people back with laws from their own ethnic background and some stolen from African countries over the years along with religion. Therefore, they have created a society that many cannot escape or be assimilated in to survive and thrive. They use felonies to keep many individuals trapped into a cycle of lawlessness and broken promises. The School systems that under-educate the masses, gave them lower skills to compete in the global market. Therefore, by breaking down the communities and housing systems to carrel people in areas that are never geared to become vibrant again.

The leadership in each city must devise an educational plan to combat the ineffective way that the children's have been subjected to by dealing with how they communicate and express themselves in education. In order to ensure that the people of color are engaged in the learning process and broken for the colonial rule of thinking black education social dynamics and economics must be taught to the children; such as math, language, among other areas must be taught.

Economics if taught correctly, is one of the greatest wealth builders, which is needed to assist the masses to rise above there circumstances. If the intended purpose of liberation is to be accomplished, the group that has been affected must control their own resources and economics and commerce that they produce. The community must work together and the public must educate the unlearned if it will survive the determent that slavery and colonialism has done to the masses of color people in each community around the world. When pressure comes and there is no outlet to deal with the problems then the value that helps to control the issues form starting must be in place to give some relief to the steam. In other words, psychodynamics is caused because there is a problem that needs some attention from all the issues life placed on individuals and if there is no way to understand what the catharsis is and how to control that emotion then other issues begin to happen. Drug addiction, unproductive individuals in the community, murder that leads to crime and incarceration.

In the late 1800's the black community had respect for self and family extended. Somehow in the early 1960 and beyond they lost respect for advancement and unity in the community and took on the pressures of the society and self-hate of their own social uplift. The issues started many years ago when the laws were not treated fair in the black community. We have to look back to gain an understanding of the reasons why? Many programs and jobs were changed to keep the black community back. It was by design and not because they were lazy, but because the establishment and the laws of the country were flipped. To keep black as close to poverty as possible. We must look at the framer's mindset and ownership then and now. How can you change the economic situation and give back what you have stolen from a group of people and give them the same economic playing field as others when you have disrespect for their uplift you enslaved?

Rulerford b. Hayes reverse the deterioration of executive control that had set in after the assassination of Abraham Lincoln in 1865. the first major act of his presidency was an end to Reconstruction and the return of the South to "home rule. The question remains did he help the situation to build a psychodynamic condition and re-route the value that would have given an emotional release to blacks in his time or did he with others condone the system. In a diary, he wrote "In church it occurred to me that it is time for the public to hear that the giant evil and danger in this country, the danger which transcends all others, is the vast wealth owned or controlled by a few persons. **Money is power**. In Congress, in state legislatures, in city councils, in the courts, in the political conventions, in the press, in the pulpit, in the circles of the educated and the talented, its influence is growing greater and greater. **Excessive wealth in the hands of the few means extreme**

poverty, vice, ignorance, and wretchedness as the lot of the many. It is not yet time to discussion about the remedy. The previous question is as to the danger—the evil. Let the people be fully knowledgeable and convinced as to the evil. Let them sincerely seek the remedy and it will be found. Fully to know the evil is the first step towards reaching its eradication. Henry George was a strong portrayer of the rottenness of the slave system. We are, to say the least, not yet ready for his remedy. We may reach and remove the difficulty by changes in the laws regulating corporations, descents of property, wills, trusts, taxation, that many African Americans will be hard to enjoy. While a host of other important interests, were not omitted to them or land and other property.

NOTES

MENTAL HEALTH CONCERN

WHAT DOES A group of individuals who were one treated with utter disrespect do in world that does not care for them as humans? When the laws that are supposed to help govern them are one sided and unjust to carry the social burdens of that group of people. Psychodynamics deals with the deeper issues that has caused problems in the life of the disenfranchised and envisages some of the problems that can help them to gain a catharsis moment in dealing with the problems they have faced over the years and even centuries. When looking at the issues the community has to understand the trauma that has caused the problems, we look at financial distributions of economics to pin a tail on the problem and issues many people of color seems to be dealing with which is not the truth. The problems stem from psychological and physical, as well mental abuse that was afflicted upon the first generation of slaves in the colonies in the Americas.

The mental abuse when really dealt with and researched by others not of that particular race can see the damage it has caused the individual who were given nothing for their service to the country. Once this is dealt with and the social and political issues have been fully dealt with then the dialogue and communication can help to bridge the economic and social problems that exist in the United States. When observing any evidence of psychosocial and environmental problems that might contribute to the communities' disorder, that data and information can help assist the police, school counselors, and other professionals as to what the needs are in the communities.

"Would Any White Person Trade Places with A Negro in America"

In the black communities there are no treatment or counselors given to the communities other than pastors and priest to help with assisting the community in dealing with this epidemic. It seems like putting the individuals in prison will help the situation and by not understanding the full measure of the problems and why the people are acting out needs to be understood. A team of individuals gathered from the churches, mosques and other social religious elements need to train others in how to identify social concerns. Slavery was a very bad social problem that created a distrust in the hearts and mind of many African American people that caused a division between the masses. Low economic wages, unequal education training facilities and housing inequalities given to them over the years after ending slavery in America. When another ethnic and social group use and abuse people, how can the mindset of those individuals deal with that treatment and integrate into a society under those rules and laws that does not fit them. How can there be any justice in the society when the land and the resources have been stripped form them.

Mental health is a real concern in the world of the African American. Borderline Personality Disorder (BPD) According to the DSM, the disorder described concerning this symptom is a pervasive pattern of instability of self-image, interpersonal relationships, and issues that arrived from early adulthood and their present life. The people who have this disorder are very sensitive to the environmental living circumstances. They experience abandonment and fears mixed with anger at inappropriate times. They feel as though others do not care about them and prone to sudden dramatic shifts. Many people with this disorder have displayed impulsivity but if the people who caused the behavior does not understand what they have done to the masses of individuals then someone has to come in and understand their pain and needs. When looking at the biopsychosocial concerns and their environment it helps the counselors and mental health providers in understanding the community and the people in that particular area. When dealing with mental health issues and problems one needs to gain an understanding of the symptoms. According to Morrison, 2006 - **Post-traumatic stress disorder** (PTSD) looks at what an individual that has been exposed to the distressing condition, which may have caused them to deal with a traumatic event or stressor (pg.269). Survivors who were in combat are the most current victim who deals with this type of condition. **According to the DSM-5 Adjustment disorder-** deals with a new change to a significant event such as war and being deployed to a foreign country. Ancillary, when a child moves into a new community and has to find new friends. If a child witness, his parents abusing one another and one of them dies, it will cause the child some relationship challenges. **According to Argosy University, 2016- Acute Stress Disorder** may occur and make an individual feel as if they have a problem keeping focused on a single episode. They begin to act as if they are not there, which makes them feel detached for society. The individual relives the moment from a traumatic event.

Overall, they all have different connotations but similar conditions, which derive from a traumatic experience that causes the individual some behavior and mood changes because of the event. So, the question is what did Slavery do to the masses of African American people in the United States. Chou FH, Su TT, Ou-Yang W, Chien I, Lu M, & Chou P, (2003) indicates that the psychologist has to use the test that will assist them in better understanding the mindset of the individual and factors that caused the problems (p.101). To describe how the individual meets the diagnostic criteria of the DSM, the position of the psychologist/ and forensic evaluator is to the understanding and nature of the person under investigation. The American Psychiatric Association (2013) indicates that if an individual show signs of any conditions then it is important to then identify the sociological and behavioral mindset of the person to decide on the treatment and requirements of that individual (p.3-4). Corey (2013) informs and indicates that behavioral oriented therapy, is an assessment tool to help identify and explore the individual psyche's mindset. The model; W, D, E, and F; The (W) by examining the persons needs and their perceptions. (D) it predicts and helps to examine the course of the individual way of thinking and progress. (E) it estimates if the method is helping the individual in reaching their full potential and if the person behavior is working for them accurately. (P) it then, predicts if the therapist must make alteration in the method and use a different interactive way to deal with the client's problem, to make them realistic (p. 97). The psychodynamic issues must be understood to gain a deeper catharsis issue beneath African American problems that need to be addressed.

NOTES

"Would Any White Person Trade Places with A Negro in America"

CAREER COUNSELING INTAKE FORM

Demographic Information:

Name: _____ Date: _____

Date of Birth: _____ How were you referred? _____

Home/Mobile Phone: _____ Is it ok to leave a message for you at this number? Y / N

Work Phone: _____ Is it ok to leave a message for you at this number? Y / N

Email: _____ Is it ok to email you? Y / N

Mailing Address: _____
_____

Career Information (please use as much room as needed):

1. Why are you seeking career counseling/assessment?

2. What do you hope to accomplish from career counseling?

3. Have you ever been in counseling before? If so, please describe briefly:

4. What are your current career goals? (Even if you are very uncertain, just fill in any thoughts that you might have.)

5. If you could do anything you wanted, what would it be?

6. Which 3-5 of these values is most important to you regarding your work?

   __Achievement   __Environment   __Leadership   __Stability   __Enjoyment
   __Creativity   __Money   __Moral Fulfillment   __Security   __Competition
   __Helping others __Status/recognition __Intellectual Stimulation __Variety   __Challenge/adventure
   __Helping society __Free time/leisure __Self-Direction   __Authority   __Independence

7. What types of jobs have you held in the past?

8. How are you feeling about your current situation?

PSYCHODYNAMICS & CATHARSIS

9. What is your current job?

10. Number of years in your current job.

11. Are you having any difficulties in your current job? If so describe.

12. What kinds of barriers could get in the way of meeting your career goals?

13. Do you have a disability for which you require accommodation?

14. Please list any hobbies, volunteer work, talents, or interests:

15. Have you ever taken a personality or career assessment? If so which one(s)?

16. What are your career goals? (Even if you are very uncertain, just fill in any thoughts that you might have.)

17. Are there other current issues that may impact your current interest in your career or in obtaining career guidance?

18. Are there any health or family issues that may impact your career? If so, please briefly describe:

19. Please describe your educational history (including the highest level of formal education you have attained and any specialized training that may be helpful to you):

20. What are the geographical requirements for your next job, if appropriate?

21. What are your income requirements for your next job, if appropriate?

Therefore, by gaining as much information from individuals it can help them to better understand their own issues and concerns while doing a multimodal evaluation on them at the same time.

NOTES

PROBLEM IN THE COMMUNITY

WHEN LOOKING INTO higher education and how problems can occur from bad information, which has been gathered by forensic investigations and criminal interviews it indicates that while there is likely to be some difference between offenders and everyday citizens regarding the prevalence rates of certain disorders, such as personality disorders, the correctional population assuredly exposes forensic mental health professionals to the full gamut of both clinical and personality disorders. This means that the mental health environment in the jails is adequately high for both men and women in the prison complex system. This mechanism identifies the severity of both mental health and how psychodynamics builds on the mindset of individuals. The question that I have pondered was how do the individuals deal with the social problems and blow off steam when things get to rough for them. Some of the common mental health disorders in correctional facilities are depression, bipolar disorder, schizophrenia, anxiety disorders, and posttraumatic stress disorder.

This is very difficult to deal with when the state hospital and other facilities have been closed due to budget restraints. The issues can come from an array of social problems that start with inadequate health care and quality of care for individuals at an early age in society. What are the children taught in the elementary schools that has led them to the pipe line of incarceration? Weinstein (2000) indicates that the main reasons are from a lack of fundamental policy and goal for the correctional mental health care facilities (p.6). The allocation of funding and resources within the facilities and institutions. The penitentiary staff is not trained to understand the broader needs of the criminogenic factors which should be given to the inmates to help them to understand their issues better if released back into the community. One of the first basic assumptions about helping the inmates has to change, by envisaging the behavioral theories that focus in on the human element to better to understand the (praxeology) causes the actions of the inmate. The opinion of the provider-client relationship is to better understand the nature of the individual's issues and habits to help them with a continuum of care upon released to cope better in the society. Psychodynamics identifies the problem, and catharsis looks to treat the problems by redirecting their emotional frustration. This comes from the initial assessment of patients from the clinical evaluation, forensic assessment, special needs assessment. From these assessments the forensic counselor can assist the counseling staff in placing the individuals in the housing to better help them manage the criminals providing they have some experience and training on the job to deal with the ones with behavioral personality issues. Drogin, E, Dattilio, F, Sadoff, R, and Gutheil (2011) indicate that the educational aspects are critical to the understanding of the prisoners and people as to, what coping skills they can learn from the environment while in the prison system (p.424). The individuals that are in prisons will come back out into society and if the mental health issues and problems that created their detriment is not understood then the same psychodynamics and issues will cause them the same problems. How does a person deal with emotional problems when there is not outlet for them to vent and harness the conditions? Personality issues are some of the most significant factors that will hinder the process in the community and the prison complex system. Fagan, Thomas, and AX, Robert (2003) indicate that personality disorders have to be understood if the pastors and mental health providers will be able to do their job and maintain mental control of the criminals while confined in their minds in a society that does not have adequte training (p.104). Drugs has ruined our communities and mental health situations have been denied and overlooked for years. The moral and social structures in the black families are destroyed and lacking male leadership in the communites.

More females are obtaining jobs and becoming the economic stabilizers in the family, which is great and wonderful providing they understand the social implication impossed on the survival of the black man. The issues of economics are built in the fabric and mindset of the economic stablizer to dictate control and minmize the males social power in the home. This is done by the rethinking of the system in corprate America. This is the new Jim Crow syndrome and William Lynch process, if you do not know what the methods are then read up on the process. This is one of the issues that black america is faliing and the process of the jim crow and lynch method has lasted longer than the intended process when it was developed.

We are know more educated and wealthy in the communites now but do not own the property, and industries to create our own economic structures. The Black community do not use or put there money into their own banks or insitution. So they can to lend to each other nor do they trust in their own self. This is a in- breeded method that slavery put in the minds and heart of the freed slaves. Dependance on another ethnic group to oversee their progress. This would not have happened if the African slaves would have orgainzed themselves and trusted in their own insitution; intergation killed the dreams and the progress in each community.

Therfore, this is the reason they have psychodynamic (Pressure) issues in the world, and the communities, they are searching for their catharsis (emotional release) moment; these are some of the reasons why so many young black and latinos are in jail and dealing with social issues and authority concerns. Mental health is another deep concern in the world that have been forgotten. Criminal Justice reform is not even in the margin and cases have been viewed wrong for years and many blacks have been convicted of crimes when they were innocent. Killing of African Americans are done in large rates and no conviction for them when a police has commited the act. These are some of the problems in the community that needs addressing in the legislation and federal laws in America. Failer to attend to these issues from the church pulpit and law departments are critical to this process. If God does not hears form us then the world we live in will not value us.

"Would Any White Person Trade Places with A Negro in America"

NOTES

LACK OF CORRECT EDUCATION

IF THE MASSES of African Americans have been given information that was retrieved in school and they are still behind the ball curve of economic success, then it is shows, how the education is being taught to them. During the reconstruction period African Americans understood that education, which was withheld from the, helped them to projected better and understand the dynamics of the pressure that was placed upon them which helped them to seek more knowledge. Even in the midst of being mentally abused and kept from education as simple as reading and writing, also simple math reasoning.

The African American people are still under the harshest punishments, but they have still risen to the top of every occasion and excelled in every challenge set before them. Benjamin Banneker was taught how to read and do math then later he taught his teacher how to understand math better. He built the first clock in London and the watch we know today. The word of God was taught to them to keep the majority of the slaves in check and lockstep for years. Telling them that Jesus was white when in fact the Bible (Daniel 10: 6) emphatically explains to us that Jesus was black. Well you can believe a lie or the truth of God's word, your choice. To further expound on the word and thought if the angel told joseph to take the Mother and child into Egypt to hide then you tell me. When you are mis-educated and believe lies over what you can read then you are the one they need to keep them in power. Wake up people, lean not on your own understanding acknowledge him and he will show you the way.

In a book called "Thou Shall Prosper" the author explains that the Jews use the word of god to create wealth and leave others behind, because they do not understand the word of God correctly. The Koreans use the west African money system to save funds and buy homes, cars, business, and educate their children how to study, and how blacks spend money and on what they spend it on. We are consumers not investors like we use to be, therefore the African American group will continue to stay on the bottom because they have lost their faith in God and self.

Education and understanding are critical in the African American world to lose sight of that is the detriment of the race and when kids who are born in this world look to see us on the bottom and a few of us on the top begging to get in then the race of another. They become confused and lose self-identity they will marry out their race and believe that their mother or father made a mistake. They become rich and then look for that white trophy rather than seeking that beautiful back Queen from the ghettos and give her a chance. Or go back to Africa and get one of them if only that were educated in self and wealth, then they would understand the struggle. In Africa the woman there are pretty, black and sexy you have to go to understand don't rely on what they tell you about mother Africa.

What you are exposed to will help you make wise decision, but if your mind is trapped in the world of another then you will be stuck. Colonialism is a critical understanding for African Americans in this country to learn how to unravel the deeper problem they still face in Africa. African Americans are taught that Africa is full of trees and underdeveloped which is not the case and they are dealing with what we have been dealing with in America for years. Our duty is to go back and help them understand how their economic can help us thrive. One, they speak three to four different languages where we in America only speak one language. If you cannot communicate with your brother and sister in Africa then how do you think you are smarter than your sister or brother in Africa. By us working together and loving each other we can build a pan African movement and help assist our brothers and sisters.

The goal of this communication is to breakdown the stereotypes between American blacks and our African sisters and brother. They are hungry and ready to work with us but we have to understand the areas where we need to do business. Our churches and members have to learn to trust God and lend a hand to our African Brother and Sisters, by buying the products they make and sell them here in our country. While we learn how to our economic knowledge with them and share how we do business with them and get the products from them to create wealth.

How will the educational system provide the same understanding to the curriculum for the less fortunate? The socioeconomic problem and the fear of African Americans being taught the correct information has to disappear before the society can work to a common goal. Most White Americans have a serious concern or some problem with the training of the African American people in America and abroad with the correct educational requirements and they control the system. Could it be because the masses of White Americans feel as though they cannot look at what they have created and deal fairly with the same people whom they have mis-educated? The mindset of the individuals has to change for the system to work, the polyglot factor (learning other languages), lets us know in Africa that they can speak different languages and what was taken from us was the ability to communicate. Therefore, the white mindset does not want to recognize the achievements of the African American people who had to deal with being use. All of the knowledge that African Americans had was used to advance the economy. Many of the experience that the African American had to endure to make it in the society would have turned the stomach of the dead.

During the time of Jim Crow, the laws that keep them under the foot of excellence, unequal school funding and the separation of the masses until the ruling of Brown vs. the Board of education, where the Federal Government ruled it to be unacceptable, in 1954. To be born in America with these struggles and still contribute to the formation of the nation says something about determination. According to (Gysasi Foluke, 2002) all these issues have a Bering on the sociological state of the African American even today as well as the society to which they live.

Religion has played a great part in the forming of the mindset of the African American in the society, and how they pulled in the information into their minds. The question that still remains to this day, is do they have the correct information from the preachers who were disseminating the information of the Gospel. In a book called *Race, Religion, & Racism* it stated that how can the church deal with these situations when the preacher are hand in hand with the slave owners, and, that not only did they help sanctioned the selling of the African Slaves into that peculiar institution, they also profited from them, according to (Price, 1999 pg 15).

NOTES

COGNITIVE THINKING

IN ORDER FOR all this to take place the African American community has to understand what they want and need from our African brothers and sisters on the continent. The brothers and sisters in Africa have been mis educated and treated bad in the country, they have the knowledge and stamina to make it in business. But because of them being colonized and not able to control their own social business it has been difficult for them to navigate through the rough issues when it comes to economics. So critical thinking has to be done with a collaboration of spiritual minded sisters and brothers form Black America to help them deal with the internal and social economic problems they have been facing for all these many years.

While traveling in the country I realized that the problem they face every day is organization and being together. By looking at the economic and social structure in the area of Senegal I found that they only need an outlet to increase their outputs. This will help them in developing a system to ensure economic success. Combining our thoughts and skills form America with the African brothers and sisters in the region will help both us here and them there. This is called verbal protocol, which needs to take place between the African and the black American before any business transaction can take place.

As cognitive science is being done the trust factor have to be in place to ensure the shipping process and delivery of goods has been established. What has happened over the years form slavery and during the occupation of Africa by others is a dissociation. It is our intent to ratify the situation and create a bonding solution that will help black America thrive economically.

Investors is the key to creating economic stability in the United States and between Africa, we must understand the dynamics and share with our brothers and sister abroad on how to deal with each other. Cognitive thinking is critical and crucial in psychodynamic and how it plays in the world of catharsis. It can and will breakdown the issues we find in the economic world and social structure of African and black American economics and how they communicate with each other.

The African has been taught to go against their own liberation and it has stifled their own economy. The problem for many of them has been caused because they have been tricked like many other areas by allowing someone to take possession of how they thought and their resources. Black America has not fully understood the dynamic and social issues in Africa. They have been mis-educated and told that Africa hates them, which is far from the truth and by going there it will breakdown, the stereotypes and social syndrome they were taught in the elementary schools and even in college. If Black America wants to change their economic status and create a flowing social construct in America then they must work with their brothers and sisters in the country (Mother Country). The issues that many African Americans are dealing with is the problems that the society has placed on the educational system. African Americans are not valued in the society and are kept in a translative state when dealing with critical matters. The society believes that many blacks do not know how to govern themselves and believe they have to think for them. This is not the case regardless of the situation African are the progenitors of knowledge and thought in many subjects throughout the formation of civilization.

The African nation taught the European communities how to use the basic elements of soap and trained them in understanding how to write checks. That was not even in the system of the communities; this they stole during their trips to Ghana in west Africa. We must understand that critical thinking is crucial in any development and African American communities need to control their own communities. Integration has hurt the development and the process.

NOTES

POLITICAL POWER

THE KEY TO dealing with the issues come down to how to control the resources that come out of Black America and then distribute the profits back into the community. This way the return on investments ROI, can be used to create political power and gain legislation in the courts. Each of the other ethnic groups understood political gain and togetherness. In the early 1700; (1702) no more than three blacks could gather together in public, (1705) if you were not Christians in their original place of origin should be considered slaves. 1712, New York establishes a law preventing freed African-Americans from inheriting land.

1721 South Carolina passes a law limiting the right to vote to white Christian men. 1741 The ordinance also makes it illegal for enslaved people to meet in groups or earn money. Other political things were going on during this time and the founding of the African Free society was founded in 1787 by Richard Allen and Absalom Jones. This shows us that we were engaged in the political movement along tine ago.

So, the question is what happen to that momentum and why have the black community lost faith and the drive to engage the social issues. The preachers in many congregations have stood by and allowed the white political establishments to control their economic means and living. Remember they believed you should not read or write, this way they kept you in the dark. To understand your power is to know your worth, the goal is to begin a self-awareness campaign and share with you the reader how valuable you are to life.

"Would Any White Person Trade Places with A Negro in America"

The information that was suppressed and kept for the children in each generation was lost during interrogation. Black people have contributed to the economic success of America for years and somehow, we have allowed the white establishment to control our political rise and economic advancements. The only way to control your community and the stability of it is to own banks and institutions that will lend us money to invest in our own economy while serving and supplying the United States. Political power and economic power go hand in hand, good credit vs bad credit has to be understood. Many African Americans are not in the political fields, or the banking fields. If they are, they get confused and corrupted about helping their own, resist the urge to steal from your people, help them rise.

This is one on the problems that white slaves law owners put in the heart of the free slaves once they knew they understood money was to cheat their brothers and sisters. Resist my brother and sister learn to help them it helps you. This is a colonialism tactic. Recognize the political moves and gel together, we have lost our language, our religion and our way. Due to this method, they divided us and pillaged our self-worth and economics we have better education and still struggle. So somehow, they lied to us again and gave us a rubber stamp and check on progress. Time to get back in the game people, individualism is messing us up, when collectivism is the key to the game.

The stock market is another way they have kept us behind, we will not understand the game, played on us because we will not take stock classes, and understand the market, nor learn how to read the lines and how to set them up to make money. In the green you win, in the red you win, so how do you lose. The money pot and the investments, going up or down can yield you some money. We have no one to explain this to us, now I have, just reading this will assist you. Your frailer to act from here is the problem. I am developing a new program that helps anyone to save money.

Political power is economic power, if you understand the game. We are not in the right fields and it is time to reshape our thinking. The questions need to be clear, if you are making money selling drugs and run a street business then you can run any fortune 500 company. Change the mindset and do the work needed to make it help your community. We need committed and honest people to clean up what they have made us mess up over the years and own property, create business and invest in products that help our people succeed.

Whoever controls the writing of the laws; controls the economic out put that deals with economic movement. Where are the African American movers of the economic distribution of the money and land development? Images have meaning to those who controls the social vision of the people on top against those who are on the bottom looking; which may be a validity and a lie by understanding self and background the political power structure can be defeated.

NOTES

BALANCING & DEBT

TO UNDERSTAND THE deeper meaning of psychodynamics and how it relates to catharsis is to deal with the problem in the black community that has not been shared with them even after slavery. The issue is economics, many African American families do not understand the term or the process. We will dive into this subject to help you to gain a deeper appreciation of movement of money. Economics comes into play when people cannot obtain what they want do to the limitation of goods and services, this turns into scarcity. When the products and goods are not available in great numbers; once this is realized the movers and shakers then separated the goods and products along with people to meet the needs of the community.

How has this affected the black community when it comes to balancing economic movement within the black community. It effects the market of who is selling and buying the products to increase their living standards. If the African American group is buying and not selling then they are consumers rather than sellers. They will always be unbalanced in the market place and kept on the bottom. In order to excel in the economic world and the community the individuals who are buying needs to be the seller of the products. Many of the communities do not have a black bank nor anyone who trains the hindered group in to how to save, invest and buy products to sell and create economic stability in the global market.

Many of the African American children do not understand other languages and customs to engage their African brothers and sisters in Africa. Nor can they speak to the changing world of finance and economics. This is one of the greatest problems in the United States when it comes to wealth and economics that needs to change. The churches are also the problem when it comes to introducing economics to the congregations by going abroad into Africa and exchanging money for products then developing a brother and sister hood with Africa. Learning the foreign exchange market helps to identify what products will sell in the market where many blacks reside. What is the supply and demand for black America to make an impact in the global? When dealing with debt we must understand how to balance the products against the debt. Such as; the demand schedule, individual demand curve, quantity demand, law of demand and not least a change in quantity demand.

African American's have to understand the needs of their community and brainstorm critical economic concerns and identify the solutions. Having social forums and information gatherings will be the key in changing the mindset of the community and hearts of the broken and lost.

When a group has been trained not to love progress, they will fight change and refuse to get out of what seems to be comfortable to them. They will deny the truth and cling to the way the ruling class has showed them to think. They will cry for freedom and fight against change and doing it for themselves. This is a form of mental slavery and Stockholm syndrome a condition in which hostages develop a psychological alliance with their captors during captivity. They will have an emotional bond, between captor and captives, during intimate time together. This happened to the slaves during slavery by breaking the mental cycle and controlling their own will be difficult but not ruled out.

The best way to deal with this problem of psychodynamics and catharsis is to understand the problem and correct them while we still have time. The next generation should not have it as bad as we have had it this was the key to the promise land concept, many blacks were told once they die, they will be in the promise land. This means someone lied to us over the years and it is time to correct that mis- nomenclature. We can have it here on earth if we pull together and change how we process the wealth and concepts that we already have within our mind. We have been trained in every educational process and modality to control our own destiny but refuse to work together. Even know while transmitting this information some black person is saying something negative while others are saying something positive. God knows were we are at but do the large group of African Americans know? So, ask the next white, you see just ask them will they change places with you and see what their response will be?

"Would Any White Person Trade Places with A Negro in America"

NOTES

REFERENCE

American Psychological Association. (2010). *Publication Manual of the American Psychological Association.* Washington, DC: American Psychological, 1.10 7-16.

American Psychiatric Association. (2013). *Diagnostic and statistical manual of mental disorders (5th ed., text rev.).* Washington, DC: American Psychiatric Association.

Argosy University. (2016). *Argosy University Online.*

Argosy University. (2018). Psychological Assessment. Retrieved from https://myclasses.argosy.edu/d2l/le/content/31298/viewContent/1666553/View

Chou FH, Su TT, Ou-Yang W, Chien I, Lu M, & Chou P. (2003). Establishment of a disaster-related psychological screening test. *Australian & New Zealand Journal of Psychiatry,* 37(1), 97–103. Retrieved from http://search.ebscohost.com.libproxy.edmc.edu/login.

Corey. (2009). *Theory and practice of counseling and psychotherapy (8th ed.).* Belmont, CA: Brooks/Cole, Cengage Learning.

Corey, G. (2013). *The Art of Integrative Counseling.* Belmont, CA: Brooks/Cole.

Creswell, J. (2013). *Qualitative Inquiry & Research Design; Choosing Among Five Approaches.* Thousand Oaks, CA: Sage.

Drogin, E, Dattilio, F, Sadoff, R, & Gutheil. (2011). *Handbook of forensic assessment : psychological and psychiatric perspectives.* Hoboken, New Jersey: John Wiley & Sons, Inc.

Fagan, Thomas & AX, Robert. (2003). *Correctional Mental Health handbook.* Thousand Oaks, CA: Sage Publication INC.

Morrison, J. M. (2014). The Clinicians Guide to Diagnosis. In M. James Morrison, *DSM-V Made Easy* (p. 228). 72 Spring Street, New York, NY 10012: Guilford Press.

Weinstein, H. (2000). *Psychiatric Services in Jail and Prisons.* Washington, DC: American Psychiatric Association.

ABOUT THE AUTHOR

DR. KEITH GAVIN

Rev Dr. Keith Gavin Born in Historical Rochester NY

Worked with Ron Thomas, who was a former city council member within city of Rochester NY. I volunteered with the **NAACP,** chapter in Rochester NY, under the leadership of Pastor Novell Goff, the Pastor of Barber AME church? Helped Rev. Dr Goff in viewing over 175 cases, and interviewed 75 physical cases daily. Made court appearances, helped to dispose of a 6 yr. murder case having the case revoked to be over turned from 25 yrs. to life to 1 day, resulting in the man and his family giving their lives to Christ, worked on a rape case, which resulted in the case being dismissed. Also, in the Greater Rochester area dealt with enormous discrimination cases throughout the city. Spent 16 years in Army reserves, 3 years special Operations Civil Affairs.

Returned to active military duty, served additional 7 years to complete 23 years in military. Transferred my ministerial affiliation to Anderson chapel AME church in Killeen Tx. While under the leadership of Pastor Walter MacDonald and under Pastor William Campbell, served several years in the **Social Action committee**, also helped to hold, the 1999 mayor, city school, and city council, forum with the NAACP Chapter of Killeen. Designed and developed a new measure for the Child Support system, for over 2 yrs to better help the community.

Developed & Created the **United Black Afro-American Ministries**, in TX, 2002. Served three years in Special Operations

94-97, two tours in Iraq, 2003-04, then returned 2004-05, returned to continue the fight for the disinherited.

Completed two years of college in six months to finish his **Bachelor of Science in Liberal Arts Degree, received the degree from Excelsior College.** Have a Diverse Major in **Sociology & Psychology & Religion**? Graduated twice from **Liberty Baptist Theological Seminary; Masters of Arts in Theological studies, and a Master of Religious Education/Pastoral Counseling.** Holds a **Doctorate in Pastoral Community Counseling (Psychological/ Behavioral) EDD, from Argosy University. Has a certificate from Harvard University in Negotiation and Leadership,** President of **Together Ministries, INC** faith-based organization? Work as PT chaplain at the Metroplex Hospital as one of the Staff. Completed Forensic Psychology Masters in Law Enforcement in 2019, created a Forensic/ Notary business in 2020.

www.ingramcontent.com/pod-product-compliance
Lightning Source LLC
Chambersburg PA
CBHW031548210526
45464CB00003B/1199